St. Patrick's Day
Holiday Coloring Book for Adults

St. Patty's Day Coloring Pages For All Levels of Colorists

What do you get when you cross
poison ivy with a four-leaf clover?

A rash of good luck.

~Author Unknown

Color Test Page

Happy St. Patrick's day!

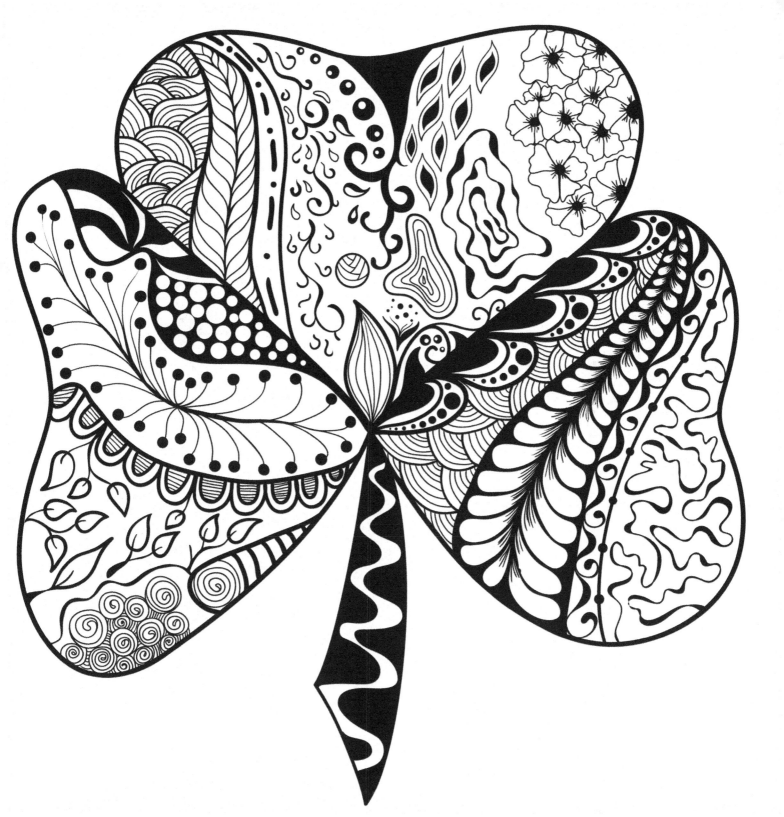

Happy St. Patrick's Day

If you're enough lucky to be Irish,
you're lucky enough!

~Irish Saying

Other fun and awesome adult coloring books available at CNandJ.com:

The Be A Pineapple
Adult Coloring Book

The Adult Coloring Book for
Coffee Lovers

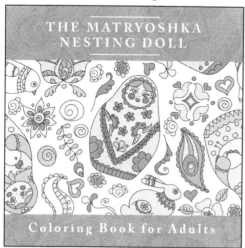

The Matryoshka Nesting Doll
Coloring Book for Adults

The Ultimate Adult Coloring
Book for Men

www.CuteNotebooksandJournals.com

Made in the USA
Coppell, TX
18 March 2021